Whispering In The Dark Journal

Whispers in the Dark/Dr. Terri Lane Hunt
ISBN 978-1-952315-90-9
Journal

Unless otherwise noted, scripture references are from the King James Version of the Bible.

To order additional copies of the resource, write Chosen Pen
Customer Service: 1420 Hoke Loop Road Fayetteville, NC 28314
Fax orders to 910-868-3300
Phone orders to 910-818-6652

Website:
www.chosepen.com
www.chosenpenacademy.com

Printed in the United States of America

Whispering In The Dark Journal

In the stillness of the night, when all is quiet, our hearts often become the loudest. It is in these moments—when we face our deepest fears, struggles, and uncertainties—that God's whispers can be heard most clearly. "Whispering in the Dark" is an invitation to embrace those quiet moments, where we seek solace, strength, and guidance from the One who knows us best.

This journal is more than a collection of prayers. It is a journey of hope, faith, and empowerment. Each entry offers a call to action—an opportunity to respond to life's challenges with courage and purpose. You will find motivational thoughts to uplift your spirit, scriptures to anchor your soul, and heartfelt prayers to guide your way.

As you embark on this journey, remember that even in the darkest times, there is light. Let this journal be your companion, helping you draw closer to God as you whisper your heart's desires, trusting that He hears every word.

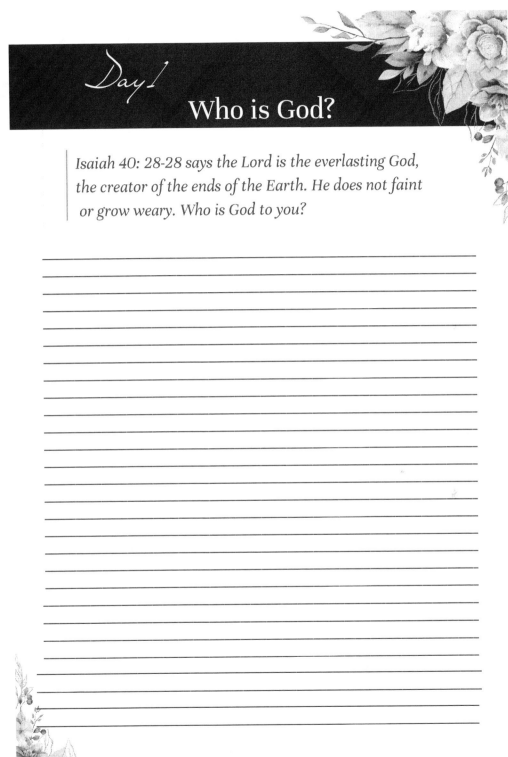

Day 1

Who is God?

Isaiah 40: 28-28 says the Lord is the everlasting God, the creator of the ends of the Earth. He does not faint or grow weary. Who is God to you?

_____
_____
_____
_____
_____
_____
_____
_____
_____
_____
_____
_____
_____
_____
_____
_____
_____
_____
_____
_____
_____
_____
_____
_____
_____
_____
_____

Dear God, thank you for being the Lord my God, the
Holy One of Israel, my savior. In Jesus' name, Amen.

Day 2
Whispering in the Dark

What is it?, it's my time when I go to God in prayer with all of my heart, disappointments and concerns. What are you holding on to that you need to whisper about? What is the (IT) that's keeping you from moving forward?

"Do not let your heart be trouble, Trust in God, Trust also in me." - John 14

_____
_____
_____
_____
_____
_____
_____
_____
_____
_____
_____
_____
_____
_____
_____
_____
_____
_____
_____
_____
_____
_____
_____
_____
_____
_____

Dear God, allow me to let go and let God. Give me faith to trust you. In Jesus' name we pray, Amen.

Day 3
Whispering as a Child

The first prayer I whispered as a small child was Matthew 6: 9-13, "Our Father's Prayer." Can you remember your first prayer? If so, can you share your first prayer as a small child?

_____
_____
_____
_____
_____
_____
_____
_____
_____
_____
_____
_____
_____
_____
_____
_____
_____
_____
_____
_____
_____
_____
_____
_____
_____

_____

_____

_____

_____

_____

_____

_____

_____

_____

_____

_____

_____

_____

_____

_____

_____

_____

_____

_____

_____

_____

_____

_____

_____

_____

_____

_____

_____

_____

*"Our Father in Heaven," when we pray we are addressing our
Father, the one who gives us life and loves us so much he sent
Jesus to purchase our salvation. We don't need to be afraid or
timid as we approach Him.*

Day 4
Whispering as a Teenager

This is when I really begin to understand how to communicate with God I did that by reading and researching and understanding God's word. How did you communicate with God as a teenager? How did you feel about God? Did you know God?

" For anyone who speaks in a tongue does not speak to me, but to God while those who has the gift of prophecy speaks to people. -1 Corinthians 14:2

_____

_____

_____

_____

_____

_____

_____

_____

_____

_____

_____

_____

_____

_____

_____

_____

_____

_____

_____

_____

_____

_____

_____

_____

_____

_____

_____

Dear God, give me the understanding of the prophecy and speaking. In Your name, I pray. Amen.

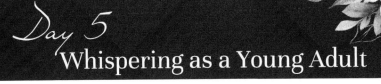

Day 5
Whispering as a Young Adult

This is when I begin to understand what it is to have wisdom.
I became more spiritually matured. That is the process of growing
in my relationship with God. It is not limited to a specific age.
It can be achieved by becoming more like Jesus Christ. It has been
said that the standard for Christian maturity is Jesus himself. James
3:13-18 tells us, The difference between earthly and heavenly wisdom
and how wisdom from above is pure, peaceable, and open
to reason.
"Get wisdom, get understanding! Forget it not. Neither decline from the
words of my mouth. Forsake her not, and she shall preserve thee! Love her,
and she shall keep thee! - Proverbs 4:5-6"

Dear Lord Jesus, teach me to grow closer to you and prouder
of you with every passing day of my life. In Jesus' name, Amen.

Day 6
Do you believe in angels?

Psalms 91:11-12 says: "For he will command his angels concerning you to guard you in all your ways; they will lift you up in their hands sothat you will not strike your foot against a stone. Do you have any Angel in your life that have made a different?

Dear God thank you for the angels you have placed in our lives to keep watch over us. In Jesus name I pray, Amen.

Day 7
My New Beginning

Romans 8:38-39 says, "For I am convinced that neither death nor life, neither angels nor demons, neither the present nor the future, nor any power, neither height nor depth, nor anything else in all creation, will be able to separate us from the love of God that is in Christ Jesus our Lord." #7 is the number of completion and #8 is the number of beginnings, I feel like this is my new beginning. My new life, I am free, now I can have peace. What's holding you from your beginning?

_____
_____
_____
_____
_____
_____
_____
_____
_____
_____
_____
_____
_____
_____
_____
_____
_____
_____
_____
_____
_____

Dear Father, thank you for my new beginning, fresh start, and peace of mind. In Jesus' Name, Amen.

Day 8

Whispering as a wife

Matthew 19:6 says, "Therefore what God has joined together, let no one separate." I tried so hard to live by the word of God. I soon learned what it was to be unequally yoked. In what areas do you need to improve your marriage as a wife? What are your responsibilities as a Godly wife to your husband? Always remember:
"It is better to live in a desert land than with a quarrelsome and fretful woman. Better to live in a desert than with a quarrelsome and nagging wife. -Proverbs 21:19

_____
_____
_____
_____
_____
_____
_____
_____
_____
_____
_____
_____
_____
_____
_____
_____
_____
_____
_____
_____
_____
_____
_____

Dear Father, please give me the strength and patience to be a Proverbs woman and a Godly wife. In Jesus' Name, Amen.

Learning to deal with Grief

Lamentations 3:31-33 reminds people to bring their grief to the Lord, who will show compassion and mercy. Joshua 1:9 encourages people to stay strong and courageous and to remember that God will be with them. Psalm 46:1-3 says that God is a refuge and strength and ever-present help in trouble. Losing my sister in a very bad car accident was more than I could handle. I prayed and I asked God to help me and there were the scriptures he gave me. How do you deal with the death of a loved one? What scripture do you use?

_____

_____

_____

_____

_____

_____

_____

_____

_____

_____

_____

_____

_____

_____

_____

_____

_____

_____

_____

_____

_____

_____

_____

Dear Father, please help me to trust and believe that my loved one is in a better place. You said, "to be absent from the body, and to be present with the Lord." 2 Corinthians 5:8. Lord, give me strength to deal with this grief. In Jesus' Name, Amen.

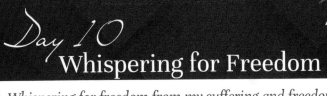

Day 10
Whispering for Freedom

Whispering for freedom from my suffering and freedom for healing.Confess your sins to one another. When we ask God for healing, it doesn't mean our bodies being healed from sickness. God will heal our bodies, our sins, and our relationships. What areas of your life do you need healing?

_____
_____
_____
_____
_____
_____
_____
_____
_____
_____
_____
_____
_____
_____
_____
_____
_____
_____
_____
_____
_____
_____
_____
_____
_____
_____
_____
_____

Dear Father, heal me everywhere I hurt. Heal my mind, body, and soul. Please heal anyone among us that needs healing in any area of their lives. Thank you, Father, for staying on the cross for our transgressions. For being crushed for our iniquities; the punishment that brought us peace was on you, and by your wounds, we are healed. Isaiah 53:5 In Jesus' Name, Amen.

Day 11
Whispering for Stronger Faith
"Oh ye of little Faith"

Ephesians 2:8 says by Grace you have been saved through Faith, and this is not by your own doing; it is the gift of God, not a result of works, so that no one may boast. So many nights I was whispering to God to give me stronger faith as a wife and a mother. I question my faith more as a mother, always praying to be the best mother and raise the best children. The more I whispered to God, the stronger my Faith became. When did you question your faith? What area of your life caused you to question your faith?

_____
_____
_____
_____
_____
_____
_____
_____
_____
_____
_____
_____
_____
_____
_____
_____
_____
_____
_____
_____
_____
_____
_____
_____
_____
_____
_____
_____
_____
_____
_____
_____

Dear Father, you said all we need is faith the size of a mustard seed. Father, that seems so small, but so powerful. Please help me by giving me stronger faith. In Jesus' name I pray, Amen.

Day 12
Whispering for Clarity

Whispering for clarity the quality of being coherent and intelligible. Psalms 119:18 Open my eyes that I may behold wonderful things from your law. Whenever there is a concern in my life, I ask God for clarity so I can better understand the lesson in that situation and hear God's voice.

Dear Father teach me how to get clarity and understanding in your word, open my ears to hear, eyes to see and a mind to understand your word. In Jesus name. Amen

Day 13

God will turn your pain into purpose

Your pain, tears, and discomfort have a purpose. Every trial, test, and triumph will teach you to acknowledge. Father God: Psalms 22: 1-5 talks about Jesus' anguish. My God, My God, why have you forsaken me? Why are you so far from saving me? So far from my cries of anguish... My God, I cry out by day. Share some of your trials, tests, and triumphs that happen in your life. How did you see God's hands at work in your tests and trials?

_____

_____

_____

_____

_____

_____

_____

_____

_____

_____

_____

_____

_____

_____

_____

_____

_____

_____

_____

_____

_____

_____

_____

Dear Father God, please teach me how to turn my pain, tears, and discomfort into purpose. Your pain and discomfort were to die for our sins. In Jesus' name, I pray. Amen

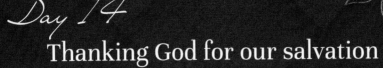

Day 14

Thanking God for our salvation

Psalm 4:1 Hear me when I call, O God of my righteousness: Thou hast enlarged me when I was in distress. Have mercy upon me and hear my prayer. David expressing his feelings to the Lord at night. In verse 8 David is preparing for bed and has a lot on his mind. I have whispered many nights for God to have pity on me and hear my prayers. Sometimes it was my job, my marriage, my children, or when I couldn't pay my bills, we can all identify David's distress.

Dear Father, you know me, you know my heart. I need your help, Lord. I need your comfort. There is trouble on every hand. Please hear my prayer, dear Lord. In Jesus' name, Amen.

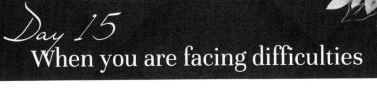

Day 15
When you are facing difficulties

Always remember: God is always with you. You can always count on Him in your most difficult times. God is our refuge and strength, an ever-present help in trouble. Consider that our present sufferings are not worth comparing with the glory that will be revealed in us! How do you handle difficult times?

_____
_____
_____
_____
_____
_____
_____
_____
_____
_____
_____
_____
_____
_____
_____
_____
_____
_____
_____
_____
_____
_____
_____
_____
_____
_____
_____
_____

_____
_____
_____
_____
_____
_____
_____
_____
_____
_____
_____
_____
_____
_____
_____
_____
_____
_____
_____
_____
_____
_____
_____
_____
_____
_____
_____

Dear God, thank you for being my refuge in difficult times.
In Jesus' name I pray, Amen.

James 1:1, If any of you lacks wisdom, you should ask God who gives generously to all without finding fault. It will be given to you...Matthew 7:7-8 says, "Ask and it will be given unto you; seek and you will find; knock and the doors will be opened to you. For everyone who asks receives: the one who seeks finds and to the one who knocks the door will be open. Are there times you feel you are lacking in wisdom? When do you experience this feeling the most and do you ask God to give you wisdom? Wisdom is the quality of having experience, knowledge and good judgement; the quality of being wise. Listen to his words of wisdom.

_____
_____
_____
_____
_____
_____
_____
_____
_____
_____
_____
_____
_____
_____
_____
_____
_____
_____
_____
_____
_____
_____
_____
_____
_____
_____
_____
_____
_____
_____
_____
_____

Dear God, you said in your word if we are lacking in wisdom we should ask. Father, give us wisdom and knowledge and good judgment. In Jesus' Name, we pray, Amen.

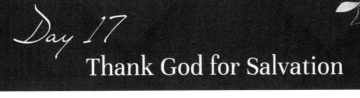

Day 17
Thank God for Salvation

Psalms says, Answer me when I call to you, O my righteous God, give me relief from my distress; be merciful to me and hear my prayer. Isaiah 12:1-2 says sing songs of praise. In that day you will say, "I will praise you, O Lord, although you were angry with me, your anger has turned away and you have comforted me. Surely God is my salvation; I will trust and not be afraid. What are your concerns about your salvation?

_____
_____
_____
_____
_____
_____
_____
_____
_____
_____
_____
_____
_____
_____
_____
_____
_____
_____
_____
_____
_____
_____
_____
_____
_____
_____
_____
_____

Dear Lord, thank you for my salvation, thank you for always answering my prayers. In Jesus' Name, Amen.

Day 18
When you are lonely and fearful

Psalm 23, The Lord is my Shepherd I shall not be in want. He makes me lie down in green pastures, he leads me beside quiet waters. He restores my soul. He guides me in paths of righteousness for his name's sake. Even though I walk through the valley of the shadow of death, I will fear no evil, for you are with me. Your rod and your staff, they comfort me. You prepare a table before me in the presence of my enemies. You anoint my head with oil; my cup overflows. Surely goodness and love will follow me all the days of my life, and I will dwell in the house of the Lord, forever. When are you the most lonely and what makes you fearful? "Repeat the 23rd Psalm for comfort."

Take Time To Pray Today!

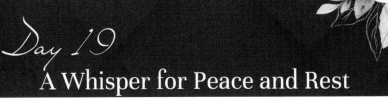

Day 19
A Whisper for Peace and Rest

Come to me, all you who are weary and burdened, and I will give you rest. Take my yoke upon you and learn from me, for I am gentle and humble in heart, and you will find rest for your soul. For my yoke is easy, and my burden is light.

Dear God, Matthew 11:25-30 says you will give me rest, and with rest comes peace. Thank you, Father, for rest for my soul. In Jesus' Name, I pray. Amen.

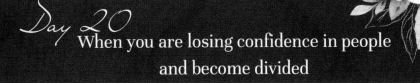

Day 20
When you are losing confidence in people and become divided

1 Corinthians 1:6 says, I come to you brothers in the name of our Lord Jesus Christ that all of you agree with one another so that there may be no divisions amongst you and that you may be perfectly united in mind and thought. My brothers, some from Chloe's household have informed me that there are quarrels among you. When you are faced with division and quarrels, what are some ways you handle it? What scripture gives you comfort?

_____

_____

_____

_____

_____

_____

_____

_____

_____

_____

_____

_____

_____

_____

_____

_____

_____

_____

_____

_____

_____

_____

_____

_____

_____

_____

Dear Father, you are not a God of confusion. Teach us, my brothers and sisters, how to agree with one another, how to love and forgive one another. In Jesus' Name I pray, Amen.

Day 21

When you whisper prayers that are narrow or selfish

Psalm 67 says, May God be gracious to us and bless us. Make his face shine upon us. That your ways be known on earth. Your salvation among all nations. May the people praise you, O God. May all the people praise you, may the nations be glad and sing for joy. For you rule the people justly and guide the nations of the earth. Share your experience when your prayers became selfish. A selfish prayer is when you don't pray for your enemies and your neighbor. When your prayers are always about what you want or need, these are considered selfish prayers. The scripture says pray about everything.

_____
_____
_____
_____
_____
_____
_____
_____
_____
_____
_____
_____
_____
_____
_____
_____
_____
_____
_____
_____
_____
_____
_____
_____
_____
_____
_____
_____
_____
_____
_____

Dear Father, Philippians 4:6 says do not be anxious about anything, but in everything by prayer and supplication with thanksgiving let your requests be made known to God. In Jesus' Name. Amen.

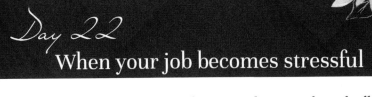

Day 22
When your job becomes stressful

Colossians 3: 23-24 says, work at everything you do with all your heart, work as if you were working for the Lord, not for human masters. Work because you know that you will finally receive as a reward what the Lord wants you to have. You are serving the Lord Jesus Christ. What are the most stressful areas on your job that you need to pray about? Working for the Lord means being diligent in tasks that are not noticed by others as in those that are visible.

Dear Father, give us a stress-free work environment. When the days or nights become too hard or too stressful, remind us that we can do all things through Christ who gives us strength. Remind us that we should work as though we are working unto you. In Jesus' name. Amen.

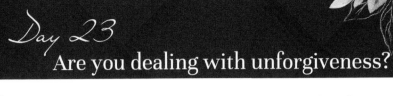

Day 23
Are you dealing with unforgiveness?

Matthew 6:14 says, for if you forgive other people when they sin against you, your heavenly father will also forgive you. Write down all the people you need to forgive and what they did to you. If you need to write them a letter and place it in your journal. We also have to forgive ourselves.

_____
_____
_____
_____
_____
_____
_____
_____
_____
_____
_____
_____
_____
_____
_____
_____
_____
_____
_____
_____
_____
_____
_____
_____
_____
_____
_____
_____
_____

_____
_____
_____
_____
_____
_____
_____
_____
_____
_____
_____
_____
_____
_____
_____
_____
_____
_____
_____
_____
_____
_____
_____
_____
_____
_____
_____
_____
_____
_____
_____
_____
_____

Dear Father, you said we must forgive people that have sinned against us so that you can forgive us. Father, teach me how to forgive, and I am asking you for forgiveness for my wrongdoing. In Jesus' name, I pray. Amen.

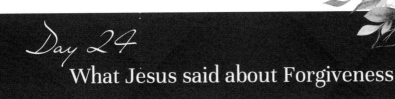

Day 24
What Jesus said about Forgiveness

Do you know the three things Jesus said about forgiveness? Can you answer the questions for those three things:

1. Lord, how often should I forgive someone who sins against me?
2. Name the part of the Lord's Prayer that speaks about forgiveness.
3. "Do not judge others, and you will not be judged." "If another believer sins, rebuke that person; then if there is repentance, forgive. What do you think about your answers? Did you learn something about forgiveness you didn't know? Explain

_____
_____
_____
_____
_____
_____
_____
_____
_____
_____
_____
_____
_____
_____
_____
_____
_____
_____
_____
_____

Take Time To Pray Today!

Day 25

How do you handle the wounds of a relationship that went bad?

Proverbs 27:6, Did you know that human words can leave wounds, deep wounds. Wounds like that can take a long time to heal, in some cases they may never heal. Think of Proverbs 27:6 with our Lord Jesus in mind. The wounds of a friend were truly faithful. Isaiah 53:5 says, Jesus was wounded for our transgressions, he was bruised for our iniquities; the chastisement of our peace was upon him, and with his stripes we are healed. Think of that friend that wounded you or hurt you real bad. Pray for them and you.

_____

_____

_____

_____

_____

_____

_____

_____

_____

_____

_____

_____

_____

_____

_____

_____

_____

_____

_____

_____

_____

_____

_____

_____

Dear Lord Jesus, you are my faithful friend. Father, you always tell me the truth about all of my sins and about your forgiveness and love. Cleanse my heart as you whisper your gracious truth to me in love. In Jesus' Name, I pray. Amen.

Day 26

What does it means to you to be loved by God himself?

List some ways you feel God's love and what it means to you to know he loves you? Romans 8: 38-39 says; for I am convinced that neither death nor life, neither angels nor demons, neither present nor the future, nor any powers, neither height nor depth, nor anything else in all creation will be able to separate us from the love of God that is in Christ Jesus our Lord. NOW THAT'S LOVE!

Dear Father, Thank you for real love, self-giving, sustainable love that originates only in you. Father, in my words and actions, allow others to hear whispers of your love for them. In Jesus' Name I pray. Amen.

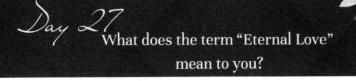

Day 27

What does the term "Eternal Love" mean to you?

Do you understand what it means to have "Eternal Love" with God? Jeremiah 31:3 tells us, "I have loved you with an everlasting love. Therefore I have continued my faithfulness to you." Even though Jeremiah's feelings were very real, the Lord's promises had not evaporated. God's love for his people was certain, sure, steady, steadfast, and unwavering. Later in his ministry, Jeremiah would write these encouraging words, a whisper from the heart of God himself to our hearts still today.

_____

_____

_____

_____

_____

_____

_____

_____

_____

_____

_____

_____

_____

_____

_____

_____

_____

_____

_____

_____

_____

_____

_____

Dear Lord Jesus, when everything around me begins to change, whisper your assurance of Love. Protection of your forgiving love that never fails. In Jesus' name I pray, Amen.

Day 28
Royalty, say it with me Royalty

Did you know that because you are a child of God, you are royalty. Isaiah 62:3 says; you shall be a crown of beauty in the Lords of the Lord, and a royal diadem in the hands of your God. James 1:18 says, He chose to give birth to us by giving us his true word. And we, out of all creation, become his prized possession. The word of God has convicted use of our deep need for a savior. The word of God has worked faith in that Savior in our hearts. How does it make you feel to know you are, "Royalty?"

_____

_____

_____

_____

_____

_____

_____

_____

_____

_____

_____

_____

_____

_____

_____

_____

_____

_____

_____

_____

_____

_____

_____

_____

Dear Lord Jesus, forgive me for so often forgetting my high calling as a royal daughter in your very own family. You are the Prince of Peace and my precious brother! Whisper the peace of your forgiveness and life to my heart, especially others.

Day 29
Growing In Grace

2 Peter 3:18 says, "But grow in the grace and knowledge of our Lord and Savior Jesus Christ." This verse means to mature as a Christian and grow in understanding and experiences of the growth that has been received. It also means to grow in knowledge and experiences of Christ which can help people enter more fully into the abundant life that Jesus offers. Some say that growing in grace is synonymous with the sanctification process, which is becoming more like Christ. This can be done by reading God's word and letting it dwell in us richly (Colossians 3:16) and by praying.

Answer these questions:
1. Am I becoming more like Jesus?
2. Am I more compassionate, meek, merciful, and forgiving than I was last year?
3. How do I respond to the hurt others cause me or I caused others? Can I honestly say I've reacted to all my troubles with faith, grace, love, and mercy?

Dear Father God, Thank you for undeserved favor that is freely given by you. In Jesus name I pray, Amen.

Day 30
Being Transformed

If anyone is in Christ, he is a new Christian. The old has passed away; behold, the new has come. The promise God makes in 2 Corinthians 5:17 lives well below the surface. "The new has come!" The Bible says, the word for new means fresh, novel, uncommon. God's creative work in us cuts to the core of our being; it addresses realities far deeper than what we wear, far deeper than outward appearances. How has God transformed you and your life?

_____
_____
_____
_____
_____
_____
_____
_____
_____
_____
_____
_____
_____
_____
_____
_____
_____
_____
_____
_____
_____
_____
_____

Take Time To Pray!

A Faithful Love

Hosea 2:19 says, "I will betroth you to me in righteousness and in justice in steadfast love and in mercy." (Luke 15:11-32) talks about a kind, loving, and forgiving father. The story talks about the Father's two sons. One of the two sons asked for his inheritance and leaves home to spend everything he had on a good time in the city. This father showed unwavering, persistent love. After spending all he had, eventually destitute, broken, and desperate, the son headed home. His father eagerly welcomes him home. The Bible tells us, while he was still a long way off, his father saw him and felt compassion, and ran to his son and embraced him and kissed him. Luke 15:20. 2 Timothy 2:13 says if we are faithless, he remains faithful for he cannot deny himself. Our father does not force repentance or faith upon us. Instead, he waits; he watches, he waits with open arms for our return. He receives us with mercy and grace no matter how long it's been since we were in his presence. Describe your faithful love to God our father and how he has shown faithful love to you.

Dear heavenly Father, you are so faithful, steadfast, and true.
Forgive me for all the times I have been unfaithful in any area of
my life. In Jesus' name, I pray. Amen.

Made in the USA
Columbia, SC
27 October 2024

44801108R00037